1

Cover Art:
'Hilo Bay'
original artwork by Linda Hostalek D.O.

copyright 2013

Moving to Hawaii, Coming Home to the Big Island

by

Linda Hostalek, D.O.

Dedicated to this gem in the ring of fire, the place of creation of new lands, with beautiful flowers, incredible sea life and endless sunsets...................

Table of Contents

Acknowledgements

Many thanks to the Divine for inspiring this work and for seeing it through. Thank you to my children, Jim, Mike, Derek, and David, and their children, whom I love dearly and have always loved and supported me, as well as helped me with this move. Thank you to my parents, Karen and Al, who gave to me the love of travel and adventure and introduced me to the tropical sea, which I love. Thank you to my partner, Reynolds, who found me in the middle of the mainland and brought me home. And thank you, dear reader, for buying this book and making this dream a reality. We are all one spirit, one family, one ohana. The love that permeates throughout this big blue globe connects us all, thank you.

Prologue

When I moved to Hawaii one year ago, it was clear
that this was to be no ordinary move. There were
many things that made this move much different from
previous moves I had made. One was the oversea
travel. Getting my pet here and my belongings
required much more effort than before, and there was
no one to help me to navigate the certain little
nuances that I sorted through through trial and error.
That was probably the most stressful part of all of this,
as I had to leave my beloved pet, Lotus with family
while she waited out the remainder of her 120 day
quarantine. If you have pets and get nothing else out
of this book, please remember to start the process as
soon as you know you are moving. It was so hard to
leave her, but the reunion was wonderful, and she has
been enjoying life here ever since.

In an effort to save others this stressful situation, I
decided to write this book to help alleviate some of
the stress associated with a move this large, and to
help one to understand some of the little things that
make Hawaii a unique place to live.

I thought living in Hawaii would be much like living on
the mainland, only with exotic scenery. I was so
wrong. It is more like living in a foreign country in

some aspects. For one thing, it is a country first, a state second. Things are in a different language. In addition to the familiar holidays, there were different ones also celebrated here!

I was amazed by things like the difference in terrain and wildlife, not to mention the volcano, waves and sea life. It has been a wonderful experience, full of adventure, but also eye opening as I confronted aspects of Hawaii that I had not even considered. I hope that by reading this book you will feel a bit more comfortable in your new surroundings, as you learn to navigate your way through paradise.

May you find the blessings of this rich land stir your soul and lift your heart. For me, after traveling a fair portion of the globe, I have finally found home. I am happy here, and I hope that you, too, find happiness in your new home here on the Big Island of Hawaii. Aloha!

Chapter 1

So you want to move to Hawaii?

If you do, there are some things you should know, which I did not, and why I decided to write this book to help others who wish to chase their dream of paradise. So, if you are ready for a new adventure and wish to adopt the island life - read on. Hopefully this will spare you some of the misadventures I had, and make the move a little easier, and the culture shock (Yes! culture shock) a little smoother. Welcome to your new life. Aloha!

Can you live on an island?

I live on the Big Island, called Hawaii. That is pronounced 'Ha-VA-ee.' The W's in Hawaii sound like V's. For mainland tongues, the names of places take a lot of practice, so don't be offended if someone laughs at your pronunciation. They are truly laughing with you - not at you. There is, for the most part, an aloha spirit here shared by all. The Hawaiian language has a lot of vowels, and you will find that many words have several vowels in a row. This can make for an interesting time trying to learn how to pronounce things.
Hawaii has a plantation and ranching culture. Although the plantations ended in 1994, there are

remnants of that life everywhere. There were plantation camps, and the large acres of what was previously sugar cane is now eucalyptus trees, houses, ranch-land or farm-fields. Many people of many races came to work on the plantations and melded into a melting pot of locals who all have their place and their culture. You will see Japanese, Chinese, Philipino, Micronesians, Caucasions, African -Americans, Hispanics and many more in addition to native Hawaiians. There is a laid back lifestyle here, and the number of cows seem to outnumber people tenfold. Although everyone speaks english, many speak pidgin, a type of english mixed in its own style. It takes a while to understand the little nuances. You will catch on eventually.

The lifestyle here depends on where on the island you are. Windward, leeward, mauka (up the mountain) or moaika (down the mountain). For mainlanders used to north, south, east and west, getting a handle on directions is important. You are more likely to hear "go towards Hilo" than 'go east.' Landmarks are important, and that will take a while to know what those are. There are two large cities on the island, Kona and Hilo. A medium city, called Waimea, (but is actually Kamuela) is in between. There are plenty of grocery stores, famers markets, shopping, art galleries and restaurants in these three places, as well as the multiple tourist places throughout the island. Most shopping if you live here will be done in one of those three places. The majority of fast food chains that are familiar on the mainland are at one of these three places, although Waimea (Kamuela) has the least amount. (McDonalds, Burger King, Kentucky Fried Chicken and Subway are the only chains at this writing in Waimea). There are many more in Hilo and Kona. That is also where the two major airports are (although Waimea has an airport which is now being developed for inter-island travel). Most people work in one of these places or in the resorts which are on the coast, especially in Waikoloa. There are many public beaches there, and some of them you can camp on for as little as $5 a night as of this writing for local residents (the fee is $20 per person for non-residents). A permit is needed though, so check if you bring your tent.

As for housing, the rents are high, and real estate is very expensive. You will most likely get your mail at at PO Box. Gas tends to run about fifty cents to a dollar more than mainland prices on average, but there is less driving, so it averages out. There is a bus route which will take you from one side of the island to the other. There are no trains, except in the train museum where the train culture that used to be used for the sugar plantations is now remembered.

The big island feels more like mainland than an island, so the chance for claustrophobia or 'island fever' is much less. The weather is consistent, but varies throughout the island. Depending on whether you are up, down, east or west determines the weather typically. Maulka and windward areas (up towards the mountain and the east side) typically get more rain. This is the side of the island where the rain forests and the lush waterfalls are. There are lots of organic (and inorganic) farms here. This is also known as 'The Hilo side." The 'Kona" side, or the west side (or leeward side) is the dry side. This airport is busier than the Hilo airport, and Kona is busier overall than Hilo. Hilo is laid back and 'chill', where as Kona is more night life, touristy, and has more shopping choices (The island's only CostCo is here, for example). There is also a lot of culture at both of these towns. It takes about two hours to get from Kona to Hilo or vise versa. Both of these towns are in the central sides of the island. The southern half has its charms (and share of cattle ranches) but much less people and no large towns. There are many small towns which cater to the locals and to tourists, and many magical places are there for those who explore (green sand beach, anyone?). The volcano is on the east, or Hilo side of the island.

Jobs are not easily found, and many people here work two or more part time jobs unless they are a professional, and have a job already in place before they get here. University of Hawaii has branches in Hilo and Kona and there are community colleges as well. There are several hospitals, but most are small. Hawaii does have some medical specialists, but true emergencies are often air-lifted to Honolulu, a very large city on the island of Oahu. This is also where most of the culture and high end shopping is found. Unemployment is high here, but many are retirees, so for them it is less of an issue. If you are moving here though, it is something to consider. Tourism is a thriving industry, so many people are employed in the hospitality industry. Hotels, restaurants, diving, surfing, spas and healing, are some of the industries that many people work in. Scientists, such as marine biologists and astronomers also have their place here.

On the big Island, being a paniolo, or cowboy, is also a viable industry. Hawaii has one of the largest grass fed beef industry in the nation (perhaps in the world). The Parker Ranch is world famous, and at one time was the largest privately held ranch in the world. The cowboy culture still permeates the island's interior, and delivers local beef to the restaurants and grocery stores here. There are multiple arenas, and horses are big business too. Rodeos are held routinely here as well.

One thing that may be different from where you lived on the mainland is the frequency of families living together. It is not infrequent for grown children with families to live in the parents house. Sometimes this can mean several people living under one roof. Many houses have other 'ohana' houses that come with the same property for this very purpose. People also vary on what is important to them in their living conditions. You will find many neat orderly houses with nice landscaping, as well as homes with hoards of stuff, including cars, tires, lumber and more in the front or back yards. Often this is not a bother to those who live there, but for mainlanders can be difficult to understand, or live next to. Many of these same people live in houses that are not up to the aesthetic standards most in the mainland have come to expect, such as intact floors, broken windows, and vermin like cockroaches and rats. People do not seem to mind having bare floors that the linoleum is coming up off. Piles of clothing, plastic bins and other items are often part of the mix. This also occurs in the mainland, and is not everywhere here. There are very neat neighborhoods, and most people are neat and orderly, but there is this one element of the population, that if one is not aware of, may astonish some people. Here the attitude is live and let live, and some people live different ways. Just wanted to make you aware.

Different parts of the island have a different 'feel' to them, and I recommend renting for the first year to get to know the area. You may find you prefer one side of the island over the other. It is a big island, and has great variety in both the landscape, weather, and the feel of the place. Giving yourself some time to explore before putting major money into a commitment like a home purchase is usually a wise idea. Take the time to find which part of paradise you prefer.

So, if you are a cowboy, or have a job lined up - great! If not, it might be a while, so be prepared! I suggest to come for a visit, then when you have decided that this is the place for you, it is time to decide what your new life will look like! And if you have animals you want to bring with - it is time to get started on their immigration right away!

Chapter 2
Moving, it takes time

You have made your decision to move here, now it is time to begin to plan on the time line for the move. You need to line up movers for your stuff, for your pets if applicable, and for you. For some, it makes sense to move your stuff and car while you are still living on the mainland if you can rent a hotel room or stay with someone else for a few weeks, and borrow or rent a car. Living things need more planning (explained below) so if you are traveling with pets, that will take more coordination with your airlines, vets and handlers. Proper planning is essential to have a smooth transition to your new life in paradise.

Getting your Pets here safely

Immigration for pets is taken very seriously. If you are the owner of a snake, guess what, you cannot bring your pet here. Snakes are illegal here, even pets, so don't even ask. Hawaii does not have snakes, ticks, or rabies, and it wants to keep it that way. The agriculture department is very busy with its inspections and does a good job at inspecting everything that comes in to the country. Dogs and cats have a 120 day mandatory quarantine, period.

This is based on rabies vaccines PLUS a blood test (no animal may come here prior to the 120 day waiting period after the test). The test can be administered and the paperwork handled by your local vet. Get this started as early as possible!!!! Otherwise, your four legged friend may need to stay with friends or family while you settle in here. If you have pets other than dogs or cats, please check with the department of agriculture and your vet for proper instructions. The animals fly in to Honolulu, and get the required veterinary inspection before they can reach their new home island. There are many little details which can derail the process. Pets need to be micro-chipped (they prefer Home first), have an approved flight crate with food and water dishes, a leash, collar, etc. These are things you would most likely have anyway. There is something called a 'pet passport' which has the pet's information and picture on it. It also contains your information. It is not recommended that pets be tranquilized during their flight as their inability to move might be impaired and could lead to injury. If you have a small pet, you may carry them in a flight container that fits under the airline seat. I recommend using a pet specialist to help with all the little details. I used Akona pet and found their service extremely helpful. Hiring this service will ensure your pet gets walked and cared for while you are not available (this especially applies to larger dogs that need to be crated). You do not want to arrive in Honolulu with your pet only to find out some piece of paperwork did not go through. The papers are time sensitive, as vets must be arranged to inspect your pet in Honolulu before moving on to the Big Island. This can be very stressful for both you and your pet, and using a qualified service can help to alleviate some of this stress. The cost is reasonable and they take care of the paperwork and coordination of flights, handlers, vets, etc. You are responsible to have the pets at the home airport (more important if you are flying your dog as cargo), or to coordinate the flight if you have a smaller pet you can hand carry. They will go over all those details with you at that time. Hawaii has a website which goes over all of this. It is very long and confusing, but it is all worth it when you and your pet are in your new home. I found this service to be enormously helpful in transporting my beloved pet. There are several pet services, I used Akona Pet, and was very happy with their service. The contact I used was named Ruth, and she helped ease the stress of moving my beloved pet. Her number is 808.937.6670 as of the date of this writing.

http://www.akonapet.com Akona Pet travel relocation services

There are also services that can move your horses, and similar rules apply (blood tests, coggins, etc). Both are very expensive processes. Love is not cheap! One girl I know shipped her horse (most agree that air is the way to go for your pet's well being) and her recommendations are listed below. Here is the list for horse transport.

http://hdoa.hawaii.gov/ai/ldc/importing-livestock/horses/ Department of Agriculture

http://www.hawaiian-transport.com/ Sheila Head Barge CA to Oahu

http://www.brookledge.com/   Brookledge, the best
way to truck a horse

http://www.pacificairlift.com/requirements.html
Pacific Air Lift requirements page

Furniture

So your pet is chipped, and has the proper shots and
tests, now it is time to prepare for your stuff to get
here. Basically, if you do not need it - get rid of it.
You are starting a new life and less stuff will allow you
more freedom. If you are going to move your
household however, you will need to hire movers.
This can be a very stressful process. I have heard of
services that basically drop off a pod you stuff your
stuff into and then the pod is moved, but that is not
how most moving services work. Moving anything to
Hawaii from the mainland is a tedious, laborious and
expensive process. It also takes a long time, so be
prepared to live without your stuff for quite some time.
Most moves will take a minimum of 3 weeks for your
stuff to arrive. It goes via truck then to cargo boat to
the dock, to the truck to your home. Often, there are
two or three exchange stations where your stuff is
unloaded and then loaded onto another truck. My
furniture had three such transfers. It took nearly three
months for my stuff to get here! Quotes were not
honored, and my stuff was basically held hostage
while a higher wage was demanded. . After many
encounters with the management of this company,

things were cleared, but the stress this put upon us was massive. Please make sure you get your quote, and double check everything! It was only because of good record keeping and many (often irate) phone calls from my partner (a former cop) that things eventually got settled. This too, was very expensive, and this was all for 500 cubic feet of household stuff. This was initially measured in a 10 x 10 feet truck with space dividers every foot. The company I went with charged by volume. Others charge by weight. I am an artist and have heavy things like rocks, easels and large tables. The movers tried to not fill up the entire space on the truck that was paid for. (They were also a day late, then two hours late on the day, only came with one man and one woman when 3 men were promised, took 6 hours for what quoted as a 2 hour job, causing me to miss my own going away party. I would of been there for another 6 hours except a friend came by and helped the movers move the heavy mattresses and furniture - yikes!). This was a series of missteps which apparently do not usually happen, but do your own due diligence and don't expect your stuff to get there anytime soon. You will be living without your stuff for quite a while, so the less you truly need to move the better. Obviously the precious things will have to be moved, but things that you can replace you will have to decide. Household good are more expensive here in Hawaii, but so is shipping what you already have. Know what you need, versus what you want, and you might find yourself a lot lighter. Items like gourmet cooking products are hard to come by on the Big Island, but plates, silverware and regular cookware is available in the big box stores. By the time your stuff comes, you may find that you did not need a lot of what you packed, or that you may of replaced some essentials you couldn't wait for. Of course, it will feel like Christmas no matter what time of year the truck arrives with your belongings. Then it begins to truly feel like home. Take what you can in your suitcases, and bring cash for setting up your new home. When you begin to take a critical look at your belongings, and what it will cost to bring them, decisions will be made and you will find that you probably do not need all that stuff anyway. But if you decide that you do, just know you will have to pay handsomely for it. It cost just under three thousand dollars to ship that small amount (500 cubic feet) of stuff. For me, the cost to value ratio was worth it, as the items were expensive, heavy, and not easily replaced. For run of the mill chairs, tables, and couches, unless you love them, it might be less cost to actually purchase new or used items once you are here. Only you can make that decision. I moved into a place where things were already set up for living, but if I needed 'things' to live (forks, plates, furniture) I think I would of bought much of what I needed prior to the furniture actually arriving. Some things I found I did not need, and are still in boxes, other things I wish I would of brought because I thought I could replace them easily here (some neat folding metal shelves, I used to have, for example). Other solutions were found, and none of it is a big deal anymore. If I could do it over again though, I would of researched the moving companies a lot better, and made sure all the paperwork was consistent. Mine had inconsistencies in the names on the paperwork (one was LInda, one Linda Hostalek, simple things, but it messed up a lot of things and added multiple phone calls and confusion, and therefore time to the delivery). As far as I know, there is not a service like they have for pets to help with your furniture, but maybe someone will create that to prevent his type of thing from happening to anyone else. I have since learned about the container shipping, and many people who move here have used their services and have been very happy, with little of the horror stories I had. The big four are Matson, Horizon, Pasha-Hawaii and Young. Many people seem to like Young, but I have not used any of these so do your own due diligence. Their information is here:

http://www.htbyb.com Young only ships inter island
http://matson.com Matson
http://www.shipmystuff.com Horizon
http://www.pashahawaii.com Pasha Hawaii

There are also pods. These are small shipping containers that you pack and lock and are delivered. I have not used these, nor know of any who have, so again, do your own due diligence, but might be a good option for those with a smaller load than that required for container shipping. There are mixed reviews, but might be a good option for some.

http://www.uhaul.com U-Haul
http://www.pods.com PODS

Vehicles

Vehicles are more expensive in Hawaii, so if you have a nice, reliable vehicle you might consider shipping it. Even with the shipping, it costs less than selling your old car and then buying the same car once you are here, generally speaking. There are three choices when moving your vehicle. Open, closed and crated.

I chose the open choice, which is where they basically drive your car onto a barge and float it over. The vehicles are covered overhead, but are open on the sides, so there will be some salt spray that will most likely get on the car depending on which position it is in. It is similar to a large ferry in the way the cars are stored. You can also have a covered space for considerably more money, or if you have a very expensive or classic car, you can crate it and ship it that way. This is also how motorcycles are often shipped. I thought about selling my car and buying another one with the proceeds, but I could not get the same type of vehicle for the money I could sell it for on the mainland. The price point difference for my car, a 2005 toyota four runner was about two thousand five hundred dollars. So, even with the shipping costs,which ran about one thousand dollars, it was less expensive. This is one area that shipping makes sense most of the time. Do your own due diligence and see. I checked Edmunds to see the buy and sell prices for the two different zip codes. Cars must be shipped with no more than one quarter a tank of gasoline due to safety and weight regulations. Just follow the rules and your car should arrive just fine. I am very happy with my decision to bring my SUV. I love my car, and it is very practical for Hawaii's varied terrain.

The same company that moved my furniture also moved my car. This was much simpler. No matter what they say DO NOT LEAVE ANY ITEMS IN THE CAR - THEY WILL BE REMOVED AND POSSIBLY DESTROYED! Yes, that is emphasized because I was told I could leave some items in the car as long as one could see out the back window. This was after I questioned why I could not put things in the car since it was going there anyway (why not use all that extra empty space, right?). It was a mainland person who told me I could fill it up to the window. I put in several small boxes, a couple of rocks, and some canvases. I also had my dog's collapsable dog bowl and fancy leash in the drivers side compartment for my convenience. I drove to meet the driver (where I lived the large truck could not go) in the local mall parking lot, and watched the driver drive my SUV on to the platform and secure it with ties around the wheels. He checked out the car, I gave him the keys and we exchanged paperwork. A few days to a week later, we received a call from the company that placed the car on the cargo boat. They noticed the items in the car, and although their policy is to destroy the items they find in the car (yes this includes the trunk), they saw they were items of value and had the decency and courtesy to call us in Hawaii and ask us what to do with those items. This ended up costing a couple of hundred dollars to ship the rocks and canvases that were there, as they needed to go via freight, not in the vehicle as I was originally instructed. (The cool dog bowl and fancy leashed never made it here though :(oh well). The car arrived in three weeks as promised. We received a call and went to the port to claim it. There is a lot of security there (think like an airport but secured a bit differently) and we needed identification to claim the vehicle. Overall it went very well and was relatively quick by shipping standards. This was shipped before the furniture and arrived several weeks earlier that it did. This came in via Matson, as does most everything that comes in to the port. Overall that was a good experience in that the price was up front (around $1000), and the car was delivered within the time window that was promised. In fact, it was actually a day or two earlier than they said, because they got it on one boat instead of having to wait a few more days for the next one to leave (I would find out the ships that transport the cars only leave twice a week or so, depends on how many cars are there to ship - they wait until it is full). I used Cardinal Movers for this as well, but in contrast to my experience with them for the furniture, this one went very smoothly, and my car arrived in good shape. Any of the above carriers who move your furniture can also move your car.

Plants

Give them away

Chapter 3

Utilities

Petroleum

You will find gasoline, diesel and even kerosene, but all at much higher prices than the mainland. The least expensive gas tends to be in Hilo, or at CostCo in Kona. Shop around. The prices can vary by up to fifty cents a gallon depending on if you are near one of the cities, or in between, like the Hamakua or Kohala coast.

Cell Phone

Verizon, AT & T, T-mobile are all available here. So is Solavei, which utilizes T Mobile towers for a fraction of the price (see www.solavei.com/starkeepers for more details).

Internet and Home Phone

Internet is run through the phone company, Hawaiian Tel is both the phone company and the internet company. Their home office is in Honolulu but they can be reached at

808-643-3456 or 877-482-2211
for more information see their website:
www.hawaiiantel.com

Oceanic also provides bundled service with internet
and cable TV
www.oceanic.com

TV Service
Both DISH and Directtv are available. Oceanic is
another provider. These are the three that most
people here go with. I would cancel your mainland
service and begin a new account here unless you are
attached to the hardware. It is less to move and less
to potentially get damaged in transit. Oceanic has
bundle service as well with internet
www.Directv.com
www.Dish.com
www.oceanic.com

Electric

Hawaii is the nation's leader in alternative energy.
You will notice many buildings, private and public
have solar panels and solar hot water heaters. The
electric company for the big island is Hawaii Electric
Light Company (HELCO), and they have three
branches.
Hilo office 808-969-6999
Kona 808-329-3584
Waimea 808-885-4605
You can go to their website to learn more:
www.hawaiielectriclight.com

Natural Gas

The gas company is Hawaii gas and they have branches in Hilo and Kona, their numbers are:

Hilo 808-935-0021
Kona 808-329-2984

You can go to their website to learn more:
www.hawaiigas.com

Water/Sewer

The department of water supply is under the county of Hawaii. It is an semi-autonomous organization. They are located in Hilo. Septic tanks should of already been inspected by the planning department. If you are building a home, that is where you will go for your information, but is beyond the scope of this work. To set up your bill for water and sewer, if needed please call the county of Hawaii's water department, Operations branch. The number is below.

County of Hawaii Water department operations branch: Hilo 808-961-8790
Please see the Hawaii county website for more information:
www.hawaiicounty.gov

Trash

When you live on an island it becomes very clear that recycling helps everyone. There is a landfill in Hilo, where the rubbish comes from the garbage collection stations that are stationed throughout the island. The garbage centers are recycling centers as well, and are called 'transfer stations.' They are manned by security personnel and is a service of the government here. Your taxes pay for it.

There are several transfer stations throughout the county. They are free and residents haul their rubbish there for disposal. There are containers for recycling materials. In an effort to keep Hawaii green, recycling containers are found throughout the island, on sidewalks, businesses and parks. Please respect the aina (land) and use them. Plastic bags have also been banned in Hawaii due to the fact that they harm wildlife and do not bio-degrade. Remember to bring your own reusable bags when you go grocery shopping. Utilizing a compost heap will also cut down on the amount of rubbish one generates.

Drivers License

To apply for a drivers license a new resident must fill out a form, pay a fee, and take a test. Some will be required to take a road test as well. Eye tests are mandatory for everyone. There are books in the local grocery stores to help you take the test. Look for them in the check out lanes, or ask the clerk. The test is given at certain police stations throughout the island and is good for ten years. It is wise to call to find out what dates and times are available, as you could drive there and find out it is the wrong day or it is too late. This also serves as an identification card if you do not drive. Only Hilo and Kona drivers license centers serve as identification centers as of this writing. The numbers for drivers license stations on the big island are:

Hilo:	808-961-2222
Kona:	808-323-4800
Na'alehu:	808-854-7214
Pahoa:	808-965-2721
Waimea:	808-887-3087

for more information go to the county website: www.hawaiicounty.gov

Vehicle Registration

All vehicles must have insurance (Hawaii is a no fault auto insurance state) and obtain a yearly safety inspection. This is done by certain service stations for a small fee, and makes sure your vehicle is safe before it is registered and licensed. Then you must take your proof of insurance, safety inspection and vehicle registration from your home state (or Hawaii if you just purchased your vehicle here) to the county department in Hilo. This is different than where you go for your driver's license. It is part of the finance department. Vehicle registration is available only at:

Hilo	808-961-8351
Kona	808-323-4818
Pahoa	808-965-2721

Cars in general

It is very important that your car is running well. The terrain is very steep in places, and some roads are only accessible by four wheel drive. Good working brakes are a must, and so are good windshield wipers. Rain can happen in seemingly a moment's notice. On occasion with heavy rains, there are flash flooding in the lower lying areas. Be very careful never to cross these as you may get carried away in the water, or end up in a gulch. The sun can damage the finish on your car, so invest in a sun shade for both the inside window, and if you do not have a carport or a garage, for the outside. Keeping your car clean and waxed will also help to protect it from the elements.

This is by no means an inclusive list, just what I have noticed most people use, or what is available. Again, do your own due diligence. Perhaps you will find a better provider for what you are looking for, but this is a good place to start.

Chapter 4
Festivals, Celebrations and Holidays

Food and music play a huge part in the Hawaiian lifestyle. This speaks to the royal heritage that created Hawaii. Traditional foods are usually home made for such occasions and are brought in a pot luck style. Some of these traditional foods are foods such as luau luau (pork wrapped in a taro leaf), lomi lomi salmon, poke (pronounced po-key, cut up and seasoned raw fish), chicken long rice-noodle, rice (always), seaweed and ferns, deep fried reef fish, amauro crab (the black ones that look like spiders), opihi (picked off the rocks on the ocean - a Hawaiian delicacy), poi, fresh fruits, jello, and coconut creme called haupio. Although Japanese and not Hawaiian, the dessert food mochi, has been adopted at most gatherings as well.

Traditional Hawaiian music, such as ukele and guitar, are frequently seen at some gatherings, people bring their musical instruments together and jam for hours. This is often accompanied by hula dancing, a traditional dance form which tells stories. After a while you will begin to notice certain songs have a certain hula dance. Both men and women do the hula, but traditionally it is a male activity (also it is not typically performed in a coconut bra and grass skirt, but rather beautiful dresses for women, and mahi**** for men, both in a cloth typically made from pounded bark called tapa, dyed with natural dyes. Sometimes Ti leaves are used for skirts as well as wrist or ankle adornments - that is mostly ancient hula). For most modern celebrations, a modern live band that plays a variety of music is often hired for the event.

There are certain times of the year that are very special. The typical holidays such as veterans day, labor day, memorial day, Dr Martin Luther King Day are also observed, but there are a few others as well. I have included some you may want to know about here.

Humpback Whale watching

Not really a holiday, but a special season that starts around november and ends around March. Peak is February. They can be seen anywhere in the ocean. You will notice them first by the little puffs of water from their blowhole. If you are lucky they will breach (jump out of the water) while you watch. They come here to give birth in the warm waters in the winter.

Regatta Day
Also known as Prince Jonah Kuhio Kalanianaole Day (Prince Kuhio Day)

March 26. Food and festivities abound, and it is a state holiday. Sometimes it is in conflict with Good Friday, since that is based on moon cycles, but the prince day is always March 26. Prince Kuhio was a cousin of Queen Liliukalani and she named him as heir to her throne. He worked very hard to help the Hawaiian people and helped to get the Hawaiian Homestead act passed to give crown lands to the people for homesteads, and wrote the bills to introduce Hawaii from a territory to a state of the United States, decades before statehood. Cultural celebrations, luaus, and canoe races are all part of the celebration of this beloved prince who died in 1922, decades before Hawaii's admission into statehood.

Merry Monarch Hula Festival

End of March or beginning of April, dates vary. Held each year in Hilo, this is the world competition in hula. The ancient and the modern hula are both represented. The festival lasts for four or five nights and hotel rooms, as well as tickets for the festival, sell out months in advance. Many people go and try to buy tickets outside. Sometimes that works, sometimes not. It is best to get your tickets in advance if there are any available. Vendors are also on hand with the best in traditional arts and crafts. The festival is named the 'Merry Monarch" in honor of Prince Kuhio, who loved hula. Note it is near his birthday (above).

Easter

Easter egg hunts and church services are held as in the mainland.

Earth Day

April 21. There are multiple ways to celebrate this holiday. So depending on your interest, you could go to the ocean, the mountains, or the rain forest. Communities also hold celebrations. Check the local paper or internet to find out what interests you the most and go.

Cherry Blossom Festival

Held the first week in May as the cherry trees blossom, to celebrate the heritage of the Japanese people. Japan is often viewed as a sister country to the country of Hawaii. Just because Hawaii is a state, it still feels as if it is its own country. There are celebrations with traditional Japanese food, drumming, chants, dance and dress. Kimonos are available for purchase and the buddhist temples are often open for exhibit or service. Mochi, a traditional japanese treat is pounded and made that day and is available for purchase. This happens in Waimea, but there is probably other locations which hold these celebrations as well.

King Kamehameha Day

June 11. Kamehameha Day is another state holiday. It is celebrated with food, festival and fun. This honors the King Kamehameha the first who united the islands and brought peace. He fulfilled the prophesies and is honored still today. Don't miss the draping ceremony at the statue with fresh flower leis. This celebrates his birthday, June 11 and the major celebrations are in Hilo and Kohala on the Big Island. The other statues of Kamehameha, which are also honored on that day are in Honolulu, on the island of Oahu, and in Washington, D.C. That day the Pa'u parade, the flower parade is held. The queen is remembered by representatives of all the islands by women who ride on horses decorated with flowers, specific to the colors of the island they represent. The Big Island's color is red, for example, Maui is pink, Koho'olawe is gray, Lanai is orange, Molokia is green, Oahu is gold, Kauai is purple and Nihau is white. The women wear beautiful flowing capes and flowers that match the horse's flowered leis. It is worth seeing.

Fourth of July

Fireworks, festivals, music and food are happening in Hilo, Kona and Waikoloa, where the tourist resorts are. There is a big bowl, which is an outdoor arena which sometimes holds concerts. On the fourth of July they often have a band and dancing along with the fireworks. There is also an annual rodeo at the Parker Ranch arena in Waimea. It starts early and is over by noon, so go early if you want to see that.

O'Bon festival

Sponsored by the Buddhist community, this festival includes dancing and food, while honoring the ancestors. Held at various times.

Admission Day, or Statehood day

Third Friday in August. This legal holiday commemorates the 1959 admission of Hawaii into the United Sates.

Memorial and Labor Day

Memorial day typically includes festivals and a pow wow honoring all native peoples. This is usually held in Hilo. Otherwise, it is pretty typical as compared to the mainland. People barbeque with their friends and family and often go to the beach.

International Peace Day

Each September 21 in Honokaa, there is the annual peace parade. This is followed by festivities at the park with food, vendors, and music. Everyone dances and celebrates peace and diversity. This has been happening for several years now and is anticipated yearly. You do not want to miss it. How wonderful to have a day that just celebrates peace.

Halloween

People like to dress up and have fun here. Children dress up and local merchants in Hilo, Kona, and Waimea have halloween walks where they give candy. Very much like the mainland.

Thanksgiving

Same as mainland, although often there is traditional Hawaiian food mixed in with the turkey.

National Pearl Harbor Remembering Day

Remembers the attach on Pearl Harbor, December 7, 1941. Honors the dead patriots. Leis are thrown into the water where the ship sank and the people died. Not a federal holiday, bigger on Oahu for obvious reasons than on the Big Island.

Christmas

Every year there is an annual night time Christmas parade, complete with lights. People put their chairs out early for the best seating. This is held in Waimea between the two shopping centers on the main street, Mamalahoa Highway.

Life Event Celebrations

Graduation celebrations

Preschoolers to college graduations would not be complete without a lei. There are leis made of candy which adds a fun touch. Some give leis made of dollar bills, but the most common is the flower lei. A maile leaf lei, which is a green vine, denotes importance, and is given as a sign of honor. It is fun to see new graduates with so many leis at times you can hardly see their faces!

Marriage celebrations

The typical wedding showers and bachelor/ bachelorette parties are the same as one the mainland. Marriage festivities usually begin a few days before the wedding. For traditional weddings, the family will make the typical food for the reception afterwards. The couple and their family will decorate the hall and the day after the wedding is used to clean it up. This is not how all Hawaiians choose to celebrate however. Many of them take advantage of the wonderful resorts to have their reception in. The couple takes their vows in the venue of their choice and the ceremony is officiated by a kahuna (either male of female), priest, civil servant or another person who has the authority to authorize the marriage certificate. The bride usually wears a flower lei, sometimes a haku lei)the flower ring on the head) and the groom usually wears a maile lei, which is the best man's job to gather for him (traditionally to cut it and clean it for him). Parents of the couple are also given leis to honor them. Honeymoons are often taken, but usually a day late if they need to help clean up the hall with the rest of the family.

Civil unions

Civil unions are also legal in Hawaii, and confer the rights and privileges extended to married couples under the law in Hawaii. These rights may or may not extend to other states depending on their local laws. Domestic partnerships are also available in Hawaii and are primarily insurance related for couples who live together. No ceremony is required for a domestic partnership. As of this writing, Hawaii is considering full right Gay Marriage, but it is still pending legislature.

Baby parties

When a child turns one year old, it is a tradition to have a large gathering, something akin to wedding reception for the baby. This is because in the past Hawaiian children often died in infancy, so making it to one year of age was something to celebrate. The family brings the food in the traditional fashion, and generous gifts are given. Birthdays in general are celebrated with great enthusiasm, but it is the first year birthday party that is the huge celebration.

Funerals

There are a multitude of religions in Hawaii, so many different ways to conduct ceremonies. For most, there is a service in a church, or a moratorium if they were buddhist, followed by lots of food and fellowship. If the person was in politics or very well known, it may be in a large public place. Hawaiian chants and poule or prayers may be said. The two are often combined (Traditional Hawaiian and Christianity). Do what the others do. If it is time to stand, stand. If others sit down, sit down too. No one will fault you for not knowing the words to the songs or the chants. If you get a chance to learn the simple songs, do so. Simple dress and respect are the keys to remember, as it is at any other sacred gathering. Honor the life of the deceased, then celebrate it.

Remember with everything there is an aloha spirit. Respect with love every one and every thing, and you can never go wrong. Life is a celebration. You can even make your own here. Go to the ocean or the mountain and celebrate and honor what is important to your soul. Hawaii is sacred land, and that echoes into everything here. Births, deaths and in between, all life is sacred and connected. Party on.

Chapter 5
Hawaiian Words - A Simple List

You will notice that living in Hawaii is often like living in a foreign land, with a foreign language. Since Hawaii is a country first, state second, there are strong native roots, including language. Here is a small list of some of the most common words you may encounter. There are many more, and if you are truly interested, you can always take a Hawaiian language course at a local college.

Here is a small sample list of some common terms:

Aloha   my spirit recognizes your spirit inside, unconditional love. Often used as hello or goodbye, but does not mean either. More spiritual and love centered from the breath, focused on the heart

Mahalo   Thank you

Mahalo nui loa   Thank you very much

A hui hou   Til we meet again

Keiki   child

Kapuna	elderly, seniors
Kahuna	a holy person who practices the ancient Hawaiian religion, similar to a shaman, priest, or priestess
Kapu	off limits, do not touch, often means sacred as well. You will see signs on land that says 'kapu' that means do not go there
Kokua	help, assistance, be understanding. For example, on a street sign with a picture of a truck, might mean no loud noises, means please be quiet or do not use your loud truck brakes
Ke Akua	The God, the supreme being (although traditional Hawaiian religion has a pantheon of gods, this is used in the same way a Christian would use "God" and means the same. You will hear that term in Christian churches
Pua	flower
Puu	hill
Pu	conch shell blown at the beginning of certain ceremonies or to gather people
pupus	appetizers

pule	(pull-ee) prayer, na pule is prayers, plural
Aina	Land, the spirit of the land
Hale	(Hall-lay) house, building,
Honu	Sea Turtle
Amakua	Spirit guardian
Haole	Caucasion, foreigner, usually benign, but it can be used as a racial slur, pidgin
Kumu	teacher
Kuleana	responsibility
Kane	man
Wahine	woman
Ohana	family
Tutu	grandparent
Okole	slang for butt
Pau	(pow) finished, done
Paniola	Cowboy
Wai	water, usually fresh water

Heiau	ancestral altar or place of worship, temple
Hana	work
Hana hou	repeat, encore, to do again
Hoku	star
Menehune	Legendary race of small beings, similar to dwarves or elementals
Night Marchers	Feared spirits who come out at night
Poi	Paste made from pounded taro root, used for many things, but especially as a compliment to fish
Nene	A type of goose. Related to the Canadian goose. It is the Hawaiian state bird
Honu	Sea Turtle
Manu	Bird
Mano	Shark
Mo'o	Lizard
Moku	Island
Mana	Energy, life force

'Oli	(O-lee) Chant, sacred, usually precedes special events
Ono	delicious. It is also a type of fish. The ono (fish) is ono (delicious).
Grinds	food ono grinds means good delicious food
Ahi	tuna
Aku	a type of fish
Kine	kind, as is the same kind, ono kine means it is the delicious kind (of food)
Lei	Hawaiian flowers, leaves or other objects, like candy or money, strung on a string, used as necklace or to honor, may also be a long string of flowers, not necessarily in a circle
Hula	Hawaiian dance, graceful hand movements and gestures typically tell a story
Kumu	Teacher, often a teacher of hula, as in Kumu Hula, full of respect
Auana	Modern hula

Kahika	Ancient hula
Puka	hole, also belly button
Nani	pretty
Malama	to take care of, protect
Keuhili	A large stick with a feathered drum type design to it. Tall, the colors are symbolic of who it is for named for. Royal areas are defined by their presence. The colors are also symbolic. You will see red ones during the Royal Order of Kamehameha ceremonies.
Ali'i	Chief, royalty
Koa	Warrior, also a type of tree with highly valued wood
Mauka	upland, inland, towards the mountain
Makai	toward the ocean

Moana	ocean
Kai	ocean, or ocean water
Kii	statues that resemble gods
Wikiwiki	fast, speedy
Huli	to turn, often seen as huli chicken, means 'turned over' as in grilled
Akamai	Smart
Kaukau	(cow-cow) food
Kama'aina	of Hawaii, often denotes native Hawaiian. Also one who lives here a long time and has 'become' local. The 'kama'aina rates' on some items, refers to those who live here currently, and can show proof (drivers license, state ID) to get the local discounted rate.
Maiki	fine, okay

Mahina	moon, also Hina moon goddess
Pono	balance, the right way, energetically and spiritually honest
Ho'oponopono	The spiritual practice of reconciliation and forgiveness

Chapter 6

Sacred places, sacred spaces

In Hawaii, the a'ina, land, is considered holy, and there are certain taboos, as well as rituals which are still performed to this day. This is only a small sampling, as a complete guide would be a huge book in itself, and would probably never be able to contain all that is sacred to the Hawaiian people. Please take the time once you are here to learn more about these fascinating deities, holy places and plants.

The mountain, Mauna Kea is the holy mountain of this land. Actually the tallest mountain on earth from bottom to top, this is one of the most holy spots on the island. The fact there are telescopes and military presence on this sacred land is a very tender subject with the local people. There is a mountain lake, where women still go to throw in the pica, (dried umbilical cord) which has fallen off their newly born child. This is to energetically connect the child with this land of its birth and the holy mountain forever.

There are many presences on this holy mountain. One of them, Poliahu, is the goddess of the snow, and is occasionally seen on the top of Mauna Kea. It is very special to have snow in the tropical islands, so she is a very rare goddess. She is also the rival of Pele, the fiery creation goddess, and there are many stories of the two of them. They keep the islands in balance. The goddess of the mist, Lillinoe is also often observed on this holy mountain as well. She is Poliahu's younger sister. Both of these presences are considered lucky and benevolent.

Pele, who resides on Kilauea, is the famous, tumultuous, fiery, creation goddess. It is said that she made her home here on the big island after being thrown out of heaven due to her volatile nature. She then wandered the earth from volcano to volcano, eventually settling in Kilauea. Other myths say she violently traversed the islands chasing after love and lust, in competition with her sister, Hi'i'aka. Some say she carried her sister with her in an egg. She is said to have many faces, and is often seen with a dog. She may be a young or an elderly woman, but always leaves an impression. Both creator and destroyer, her myths are many and varied. Her brother is the shark god, Komoho, her father is Kane, and her mother is Haumea (one version). Kane offered her hand in marriage to the war like boar-god Kamapu'a in an attempt to try to tame Pele's violent nature, but she fled. After attacking Kamapu'a, she eventually married him and they fell madly in love. Their child, Opelu, is the god of thieves and doctors. Please take the time to learn about Pele, and her myths. It is a must to go to the volcano, where she lives. When the lava flows to the sea, all the elements of creation are present. New land is being created daily by this incredible sacred process. What an honor to live on this land of creation.

The ocean is held in especially high regard. People have been dependent upon the sea since the beginning. There resides many amakua, or spirit guardians, such as turtles, (honu), sharks (mano), whales (Kohola, palaoa) and dolphins/porpoise (Nai'a, nu'ao), trigger fish (humuhumunukunukuapua') and many more. Turtles are held in high regard as representations of the goddess Kaiula, who turned herself in to a green sea turtle to play with the children (keiki) she wanted to protect. There is a black sand beach where she is said to still come out and play with the children, all while looking after them.

There are sacred bays, tide pools and thermal ponds, each one sacred in its own way. There are too many to list, just be aware that any body of water you enter has holy energy of some kind. Please respect the waters and all the life within them.

Because of this high regard for the sea, many heiaus are built near the shore. Heiaus are temples, or temple complexes, built for many sacred reasons. Below is a listing of some that you may want to know about. There are many other ones; some have no known name, while others are well known and named. Some are cared for by local families for generations. They are considered holy structures, and it is bad manners to just go in without permission. If it is a public heiau, please be respectful during your visit. These are sacred places full of history. Heiaus are typically built of volcanic rocks and make enclosures that are used for traditional ceremony, such as hula, chanting, and prayers. This is done to honor the ancestors and guardians, and to keep the mana (life force energy) intact.

The Puukohola heiau is a heiau on the coast near Spencer Park Beach Park. It is in the shape of the whale, and is a very holy spot where Native Hawaiians conduct ceremony each August. Some of these ceremonies are open to the public, but many are done in private. It is kapu (forbidden) to go in to those holy places or to the ceremonies without permission. At this particular heiau there is also an additional heiau under the sea dedicated to the shark god, Kamoho, a brother of Pele and a guardian god of the islands. This was one of King Kamehameha's amakua, or guardian spirits, and he built this temple in the sea to honor him. This was also a sacrificial heiau, and where the future king would lure his rival to his death, and become the clear ruler over the island nation. This is considered by many where the unity of the Hawaiian Islands was achieved. There is a lot of information here at this revered site and it is worth going to to learn and to absorb the mana of the site.

Puuhonua is the known as the 'City of Refuge' on the south Kona shore. This was a sanctuary ran by Kahuna (shaman/priests), one of six that were once on this island. Due to the kapu system, breaking of certain laws were punishable by death. If someone broke the law, and made it to one of these refuges, their life would be spared. These laws could be things like a common person being in the shadow of the chief, or eating the wrong food. There was a caste system and this was enacted to keep the balance as it was understood at that time. The punishment for breaking the laws was death. The bones of 23 high chiefs were once housed here, and the mana still exudes from this site. Please be very respectful when you are here. This is sacred ground where forgiveness was given and life restored. Kapu was enacted to keep the balance of sacredness. This heiau was for the sacred act of forgiveness and redemption.

Also in Kona, was the personal heiau of King Kamehameha. On the land now housing the King Kamehameha resort, the small structure there was his private heiau until his death in 1819. This place is also called Kamakahonu, the eye of the sea turtle, and is considered hallowed ground.

Also in Kona are heiaus dedicated to surfing and martial arts. There is also a royal palace there. The genealogy of the royal lineage is on display there, as well as many other objects and artifacts.

On the northwest tip of the island, on the Kohala coast, the Mo'okini family has taken care of a heiau for 16 generations. This is the heiau of Mo'okini, which legend says was built in a night from basalt stones carried hand to hand in a human chain of 15,000 men. It is said that this is where King Kamehameha was born as Haley's comet appeared overhead. This was a place of fasting and prayer in preparation for war. Thousands of human sacrifices were offered here, to keep the balance and order on this remote land. A large stone, around 8 feet wide with a depression in it precedes the temple. This is where the flesh was removed from the bones of the sacrificed. It is called the pohaku-holehole-kanaka. This parcel of priestly and political power retains the mana of a society who was willing to sacrifice in order to retain the order they created. The sacredness of this place continues to permeate the land to this day.

Also in the district of Kohala, in Kapaau, is the original statue of King Kamehameha. This is in honor of this area being his birthplace. Being the most revered king, due to the prophesies that came true regarding his unification of the islands, his statue is highly venerated. This is considered sacred ground, and as such, each June 11 on King Kamehameha day, the annual draping ceremony takes place there to honor him and his legacy, as well as the legacy of Hawaii in general. This is the original statue. There is a replica statue in Hilo as well (there are also statues in Honolulu and Washington D.C.) where the draping also takes place on that same day. The famous 'Naha Stone' which weighs over seven thousand pounds is also on display in Hilo in front of the library. This is the famed stone that King Kamehameha overturned as part of the prophesy that he would one day be king, and bring unification to the islands. The draping ceremony is when many flower leis and garlands are lifted ceremoniously unto the statue. This is followed by a flower parade on that same day, with women riding on horses, all dressed up in flowers to represent each island in the chain. It is a very beautiful cultural event, often with hula, chants and prayers as well.

There is another Heiau on the western coast in Kealakekua Bay State Historical Park called Hikiau Heiau. This sacred temple terrace is said to have been dedicated to many different gods over the years, such as the war god, Ku and the fertility god Lono. This makes it both a sacrificial temple as well as an agricultural one. This was important in the Makahiki festival, associated with abundance of agriculture. It was during this festival that Captain James Cook arrived on that spot in Kealakekua Bay. The date was January 17, 1779. The timing of his visit, coupled with the looks of his ship's mast and sails, led the

Hawaiians to possibly believe he was an incarnation of Lono, the fertility god. He was honored in the Heiau, while the crew kept journals of this encounter on board. They left on February 4, 1779, but returned a week later due to a broken mast. Although relations were good in the past, this time tensions erupted when one of Captain Cook's row boats was allegedly taken by a Hawaiian. In turn, Captain Cook attempted to take the community's ruling leader, Kalaniopuu, hostage. This resulted in Captain Cook's death on February 14, 1779. Here, life and death intertwine, just like the war and agricultural gods whom this heiau was dedicated to. The energy of transformation continues to be present here.

Everything in Hawaii is sacred. In addition to sacred places, there are also other sources of sacredness. Remember everything radiates the life force, mana, so all is considered sacred.

Certain flowers, herbs and plants are sacred and have special meaning to the Hawaiian people. The Ohia tree,for example, with its' Lehua flower is considered sacred, as is the red hibiscus, which is the official flower of the island. Ava,Awa, or Kava, is a ceremonial drink, previously only used in ceremonies by royalty. It is now available to all people. It contains kava-lactones which induce a state of focused relaxation. Kava bars are now available for those who wish to sample this brew. Maile is a vine used to make a lei which denotes honor. The maile leave leis are often seen on grooms at weddings, and for important dignitaries or other people of honor. The blooms of certain plants, such as pikake, are used in leis and have a very intense beautiful scent. As such, these leis also denote honor, due to their high cost and the amount of labor that goes in to creating these works of art. Olena, also known as turmeric, is used in Hawaiian remedies and is a wonderful anti-inflammatory. It is sometimes paired with Awa (Kava, Ava). The oil of the kukui nut, macadamia nut, and coconut also have healing and restorative properties. A kahuna skilled in the art of plant medicine can direct you to the remedies which are appropriate for you. A skilled practitioner can read the energy of the person as well as the plant, leading to the proper healing mixture for the person. This is only a very small sampling, but I think you get the idea.

Ti leaves from the Ti plant are used to purify. You will often see them used as skirts for hula, and as wrist or ankle adornments. They are more than decorative, however. When worn for authentic hula, which contains much energy, it protects the participants from absorbing negative energies of the audience, or of the energy of the story being told.

Taro is another example of a holy plant, but one that deserves special recognition. Taro is a food plant, used to make poi, and the leaves are used in lau lau (they wrap the meat and vegetables together) and other traditional dishes. Legend says the Hawaiian people originated from the Taro plant, and it is considered an ancestor. The leaves, which are heart shaped, branch out, and they come from wet ground. The best quality taro comes from Waipio Valley, the valley of the kings.

Waipio valley is one of the most sacred places on the entire island. It is said that this is where kings and kahuna were trained and lived. There is a quality of magic down in the valley, where taro fields thrive in the river runoff from the multiple waterfalls that keep the valley lush and green. A mile long black sand beach is a local haven, and is a very popular place for recreation. The sacredness of the valley, however, is unmistakeable, and is not frequently traveled into by those other than locals. A four wheel drive is an absolute must. The road that takes one down to the valley was not originally meant for cars, and is very steep. The road to the beach is very hazardous, but the magic of the place makes up for the difficult trek there. There is very large boulder on the way down, where it is customary to ask permission of the guardian spirits of the land for safe passage. There are also burial sites on the beach area, which are marked. If you go there, please have the respect for this sacred area.

Green sand beach is another interesting place and probably the only place in the world where the sand is actually a light olive green. That too, requires a four wheel drive vehicle, although horseback or a dirt bike might actually be more appropriate. It is a long walk in, but many people walk it daily. This is near south point, the most southern point in the United States. A place of special beauty, whales are often seen here when in season. It is not easy to get to, but it is well worth the effort.

The Puu Loa Petroglyphs are images carved into the lava in a flow near the southeastern coast. It is thought they were made approximately around 1200 A.D. Native Hawaiian will sometimes put their children's pica, or dried umbilical cord, into one of these holes to energetically connect the child to the land, much the same way as some will do with the pica in the mountain lake on Mauna Kea.

Lava tubes are other sacred placed where the energy of creation is felt. Here is where hot lava has flowed through the middle, while the outside of the flow cooled, forming tube like tunnels. These tubes have the essence of Pele. One can be found in Hawai'i Volcanoes National Park, called the Thurston Lava tube. Pele's essence is known to be there, and this author has felt her presence there, as well as seen her multiple faces at this sacred site.

There are also many sacred waterfalls in Hawaii. Some, such as Akaka Falls, and Rainbow Falls, are famous and touristy, but there are numerous others that have only local names. It is one of the benefits of the rainy side of the island, and why one may see numerous rainbows on any given day.

This has been a very small sampling of some of the sacred sites in Hawaii. Please explore and find more of those places that speak to you. With over 22 climates on the island, there is sure to be a place that calls to you. Go, respect, and integrate yourself in to this holy landscape of beauty and love. Your spirit will thank you. bless

Chapter 7

Wildlife of the Island

There is a variety of wildlife in Hawaii, but it is probably a different mixture than what you are used to if you come from the mainland. Mainlanders know that danger can lurk in the form of biting insects, poisonous snakes and plants, large carnivores, and certain weather phenomenon. There are a few creatures to be wary of, but for the most part, there is little to harm humans from the wild creatures.

Mammals

One thing you may notice after you move to the Big Island, is the apparent lack of wildlife, as compared to the mainland. It is not quite as barren as it may at first appear. At times, it may seem as most of the 'wild' animals are escaped farm animals, as wild goats, pigs and chickens are common. There are also wild sheep, wild cows, wild horses and wild donkeys. Feral dogs and cats and also widely seen, as are mice, rats and mongoose. There are no deer, wild rabbits, squirrels, raccoons, or skunks like you may be used to on the mainland. Some of the other islands have deer and rabbits, but not the big island. Due to the vast plains that used to be sugar cane, there are plenty of acres for small mammals to thrive, and to grow to a large size. I once saw a rat here that was much bigger than I was used to seeing in the midwest. It was nearly cat sized. There are few predators here, save the mongoose, raptors and feral cats. The mongoose was imported to deal with rats, but their circadian rhythms are out of sync, so cats are more effective at controlling the rodent population. There are bats here also, but most of the wild mammals are sea mammals.

The sea mammals, or those with a close tie to the sea, include the endangered Hawaiian Monk Seal. A large, light brown, beast, if you see one sunning on a beach, do not disturb them. Not only are they a protected species, they have very large teeth! There are also many varieties of Cetaceans. These include dolphins and whales. It is always a thrill to see one of these large majestic mammals, and people travel here from all over the world to try to catch a glimpse of these magnificent creatures. Some you may see include sperm whales, beaked whales, pygmy whales and even blue whales! The humpback whales are usually seen in the winter, and every so often a killer whale, an orca, will also make their way to the islands. This is rather rare, and when it does happen, typically they are seen on the eastern side of the island. Various dolphins, such as spinners, spotted, striped and rough toothed dolphin, make their home in the Hawaiian seas. Many people go to certain bays early in the morning in an attempt to see the dolphins. The locations they are at will vary. Please exercise caution if you choose to swim in the same location as dolphins, and do not touch them. Spiritual and beautiful creatures, they are still wild and should not be interfered with in any way. Please enjoy all the sea mammals with a healthy dose of respect.

Birds

There are many different types of birds on the Big Island. The type of birds one may see will depend on where you are on the island. Due to the variety of terrain and ecosystems on this island, I recommend getting a bird book to help distinguish the different varieties of birds. Some are common, and seen most everywhere, like the sparrow, cardinal, or mockingbird. The official bird of the Big Island is the Nene, a type of goose. There are many birds like ducks, turkeys, chickens, pheasants, jungle fowl, peacocks, and quail, which are wild and come in many different varieties and subtypes. Some are large, some are small, and they come in many different colors. Some have long tail feathers and striking plumage. You will often see these at the side of the road near undisturbed fields and gulches (ravines). The bird population is making a comeback after years of pesticides diminished the population during the sugar cane plantation era.

Pigeons and doves also make their home here, as do parakeets, and some parrots. Sparrow, cardinals swifts and larks are also found here. Mockingbirds are very common, and are known by their brown body with bright black and white markings on their wings. Meadowlarks and blackbirds are also residents here. In the pastures one will often see white ibis on the ground or riding on backs of cows. It is a fun site to see.

There are raptors here too, like the owl and osprey. Hawks, eagles and kites are also observed here. These majestic birds are a treat to see. Many people believe the owl is an amakua, or spirit guardian, and is especially well regarded. They feed mostly on fish, but also small mammals, such as rodents and other small animals. Caracas and falcons also make this their home. They are differentiated from the other raptors by hunting with their beaks instead of their talons. You will find falcons where there are large cliffs to dive-bomb their prey.

Also near the water you will find albatrosses, loons, grebes, shearwaters, petrols, and other water birds. These birds come in all different sizes and colors, although most are brown, gray or white. Some have markings, such as the Grebe, which looks a bit like a small goose with a mask, while others are all one color, such as the shearwaters, which are a grayish brown. Tropic birds, are slim and white, with long white tail feathers, and black markings on the wings and head. Herons, frigate birds, boobies, and cormorants are other sea birds that make their home here.

Cranes, coots, sandpipers and snipes are hiding in the wetlands, and terns are near the sea. On a rare occasion, one may be able to observe a puffin, a cute bird that looks in some ways similar to a penguin, but they are not related to each other. Other wading birds are stilts, and in the open country one can find plovers.

There are birds with curved beaks called honey creepers. There are no hummingbirds here, so they may pollinate the long flowers in a similar way as hummingbirds do on the mainland. There is a cute little green bird called Akeekee, which is small, chubby, songbird. It is very sweet and not widely seen. There are also little grey, black and white small songbirds with a red head on top, which you will see begging for a meal where humans go. They are a type of red crested cardinal, which is smaller than the all red northern cardinal, which also lives here.

As you can see, unless you are an ornithologist, these are just a bunch of names of birds. Get a good reference book, or look up birds of Hawaii on Google.

Reptiles and Amphibians

Hawaii has a total ban on snakes of all kinds, including pets. In the past, some exotic reptilian species have made their way here and established themselves. Sometimes to the detriment of the local population. Hawaii's climate is perfect for reptiles and amphibians, due to its warmth and rainfall, at least on the rainy Hilo (east) side. There have been many species introduced that now make this their home. Some of the amphibians are giant cane toads, bufos, which are brown, and about a foot around! They come out at night and feed on insects. There are also American bullfrogs and 'regular' frogs. There are many types of tree frogs too. Some 'poison arrow' frogs have been imported, which are colorful and very tiny, and are only rarely seen. The one you will hear about - and hear in general - is the coqui frog. Coqui frogs were introduced by accident, and are known by their loud song 'co-kee,' that sings in unison throughout the night. This mating call can keep some people up due to the volume these tiny creatures project. A small, brown, non-discript frog, once established, they are hard to get rid of. Fortunately, they are a favorite food of the feral chickens and jungle-fowl, and they tend to keep the population at bay, at least in the Hamakua and Kohala regions, where they are still present but manageable. They are very loud in Hilo and Puna. Inspect any plant you may buy from that side if you move it anywhere else. They are small, brown and easily missed if you do not inspect the plant and its soil.

There are also many vibrant green geckos with rainbow colors on their backs. They are are all over the island, except in the high country. The vibrant green one with colorful stripes and spots that you will see the most is called gold dust day gecko. They are active during the day, and have a knack for finding their way into ones home. Although harmless, do not encourage this as they leave excrement which can damage electronics, as well as it being unsightly and unsanitary. Other geckos are yellow, gray, or green and most come out at night. You will hear them 'click, click' if they are around. They feed on insects. A variety of skinks, chameleons and turtles are also present.

Insects

The population of insects is similar to mainland insects, as there are flies, mosquitoes, knats, bees, wasps, moths, and butterflies. There are a variety of beetles and roaches, and cock-roaches, which grow to a very large size. They like dark, damp places and will come out at night. They are a favorite food of geckos. The surprising thing to me is how big they grow here. They feed many of the local wild bird population too, so things are kept in balance. There are a few places where small scorpions are found, but that is mostly dry side beaches where people rarely go. There are many spiders, but although some may look menacing, they are not poisonous. The thing to look out for on this island is the centipede. Truly a frightening looking creature, they do bite and when they do, their sting can cause swelling, pain and malaise. They like to live in damp underbrush or in junk piles near the house. Please keep your area clean and check your shoes if you leave them out overnight. They are scary looking, but this is one time that looks equal the danger present. They have many legs and segmented bodies. There are 'red' ones and 'blue' ones, although that just refers to their appendages, not the entire body. Other interesting insects include walking sticks, praying mantis and stag horn beetles. These are not dangerous, but rather a nice treat when they pass your way.

A natural mosquito repellent to try is lavender, rosemary and catmint all in a base oil of macadamia nut or another nut oil. It is non-toxic and keeps the bugs at bay while you still smell nice. Vanilla is another oil to add to the mix as well, but is much more costly than the others. Light colors also help to be bite free.

Invertebrates

Unexpected encounters with invertebrates can make for a bad day. This is especially true for sea urchins and jellyfish. The box jelly fish and the portuguese man of war are the main jellyfish to watch out for, as their tentacles contain stinging cells which can not only sting, but the venom can cause systemic systems like trouble breathing, leading to death. Other jelly fish can also sting, but rarely result in the problems with breathing and circulation that encounters with these two can cause. The weather report will indicate if they are likely to be present at beaches The spiny sea urchin is seen throughout the island waters. It delivers its venom through its many black spines. Use caution, and be aware of your surroundings. If you are to go in the ocean, please be aware of the risks and dangers involved. Corals, stingrays, sharks, rip tides and other dangers lurk in the mysterious beauty of the sea. Be respectful and mindful as you enter this enchanting world.

Chapter 8

Being Mindful Matters

The beautiful land of Hawaii has few dangers, but those dangers are very real and it is important to be mindful of these dangers. It can make the difference between a very good day, or one you wish had not occurred.

This is a living land with new land being formed daily. Remember lava is very sharp and on certain locations there could be a lava tube underneath the seemingly stable surface. If there has been a recent flow, even though the top may look black, cool and safe, it could be thousands of degrees underneath. Use caution.

A word of caution: in some of the streams is a parasite called leptospirosis. It can cause a flu like illness, but is easily avoided by not drinking directly out of the waters. Again, be mindful.

Another thing to be mindful of is the weather. Flash floods can occur at anytime the rains come and the water rushes down the gulches or in to the streams. This can make the water level rise rapidly, leading to injury or death. Hurricanes are also possible here, as are tsunamis, but there is typically plenty of warning before these rare events hit the island. Most tend to miss it partially or entirely, but it is alway best to be prepared and mindful of your surroundings at all times.

Some plants in Hawaii are poisonous. Most plants give Hawaii its beauty, lushness, foods, and scents. No plant will ever go out of its way to harm you. Of the toxic plants, some have fruits which mimic fruits that are edible, while others have poisonous sap. If in doubt, ask someone who knows, or just do not eat it. Some plants will make one sick until a certain process, such as cooking to a certain temperature, has been achieved. There is no poison oak or poison ivy, but one can always run the risk of being allergic to a certain plant and getting a reaction which may result in a rash. The beautiful plumeria tree has a milky sap which is toxic, so if you pick a flower, be careful not to get the milky substance on you,and do not eat it! There are some tropical plants which are also toxic, such as the dumb cane, dieffenbachia, and various rubber trees. Basically do not eat the plants unless you know them to be safe. Most are, but be safe.

An unique hazard of the island is the presence of Vog. Vog is volcanic fog, and is the fog containing the chemicals released when the volcano is erupting. It has an acrid smell. The mostly prevalent trade winds usually carry it safely away, but at times the level is such that some people will have burning in their eyes or nose, and some may have breathing problems, or a worsening of their asthma. Some just feel more tired. It is an aspect of living on an island that is still being created. You can call 808.885.7143 for a Vog update index. If you have problems, go inside. This is similar to pollution indexes in heavily polluted cities which can also affect the air quality.

Wildfires occur at times, more frequently on the dry side of the island, and on occasion a water spout, or water tornado will occur. Tornadoes are extremely rare on the island. Earthquakes are encountered frequently, but most are small tremblers. There is always the possibility of a large shaker, and as a new resident, you should familiarize yourself with the nuances of living in a earthquake prone zone. Small things, like making sure your water heater and tall, heavy furniture are fastened securely to the wall with straps or other means, may save you headaches (and dollars) in the future should a large quake hit. Always have a plan.

Tsunamis are one more aspect of the ring of fire. Being the gem in the middle of the ring, tsunamis are possible from any direction. They can come from earthquakes as far away as south America, Alaska, Japan, or the south Pacific. There are tsunami warning sirens and directional signs to know how high up to evacuate in the case of tsunamis. They have hit this island before, and there are markers where this feat of nature took lives without warning. Today we typically have ample warning, and tsunami evacuation zones are clearly marked. Like earthquakes, the water levels are also constantly measured for both warning and for educational purposes.

One thing one does not typically associate with Hawaii is snow. When snow does occur on the top of Mauna Kea, it can be very dangerous. Blizzards can occur, and the roads are steep, so the rangers will make you leave if conditions are not safe. Listen to them and leave, the snow will cease past a certain elevation. It is fun, however, to go to the mountain during light snow and have a snowball fight or make a snowman, and then come down and go to the beach. It is one of the few places in the world where one can descend from 14,000 feet to sea level in just a couple of hours.

Chapter 9
Life's a Beach

Being an island surrounded by water, there are multiple beaches and state parks. Some have sand and are good for swimming, some are rocky, and some are reefs. Many are made from lava. From high sweeping cliffs to sandy beaches the terrain is varied and diverse. The sand color varies from white to yellow to red to green to black. The waves also vary depending on where you are on the island and the prevailing weather patterns. You may frequent one beach if you wish to swim or snorkel and a different beach if you want to surf. There is a surf report on the weather report. People will typically surf along the east side of the ocean. Being on the east, or windward side, the surf is typically larger than on the leeward side. Along the coast, north of Kona, is where the sandy beaches with the white or yellow sand are located. The resorts are also there, and the beach parks are frequented by tourists and locals alike.

If you are on the northern tip of the island and proceed south and west down toward Kona, you will encounter a number of popular beaches for swimming,snorkeling, kayaking, and all around water fun. On the north eastern portion of the island, the beach parks Spencer Beach Park (located next to the Pu'ukohola Heaiu), Hapuna beach park, and 'Beach

69', also known as Waialea, are located. The Waialea, or beach 69, beach park is sweet as the right half is sandy and good for swimming, and has shade trees. The left half is rocky and has a coral reef, so is a popular place for snorkeling. All of these parks have facilities such as restrooms, showers and changing facilities. "A Bay' just down the coast also has calmer water for swimming, this beach is located by the Outrigger Hotel.

There are beaches at the hotels that are also accessible to all by driving in the Mauna Loa gate towards the hotels. At the guard house, you can get a map which will take you to either the hotel beaches, or to mau mai, a small, private white sand beach off the beaten track. It is a lovely little local place. You park your car up, and walk down to the beach. There are no facilities here, so make sure you bring what you need, including plenty of water, and also that you bring anything you brought in out with you again. Rocky to the left and right, but with a sugar sand middle, it is picture perfect. The waves are usually gentle here. It is a lovely place to spend an afternoon.

There are some other beach parks as one proceeds down the road to Kona. Kukio beach at the four season resort is beautiful, and turtles are often seen here. The beach is rocky and not well suited to swimming. One can spend some time and have a drink at the sea side bar at the four seasons while you watch the waves. Be prepared to spend extra for that scenery though, as the drinks are expensive. Another beach park is called Kua Bay. It has nice paved roads and full facilities. Two parks further down the road are called Kekaha Kai and Makalawena. Both are rough private getaways with no facilities or lifeguards. Do not attempt without a four wheel drive vehicle. The gate is locked by 7pm, so plan your activity accordingly.

Kaloka-Honokohau National Park and beach includes restaurants and grocers. Port-a-potties on the beach, with full facilities, including showers, at the marina. Further down the coast, as one approaches Kona, even the old airport has been turned into a beach. It has lovely gardens and is kid friendly.

On the Kona side, there are multiple beaches, places to surf and to just hang out. King Kam beach is in the middle of Kona, as is White Sands, also known as magic sands due to the sand sometimes 'disappearing' only to return a few days later. This is a favorite in town beach, but not one for swimming. There are many restaurants on the shore, and many good beach parks south on the main drag down a way.

There are places to go snorkeling, complete with showers and facilities, including picnic tables, such as Ho'okena Beach Park (no lifeguard) and Kahaluu Beach Park (lifeguard present). Two step beach and Manini beach are also located this side. Most of these are good to swim or snorkel, just be mindful as most have no lifeguards.

Further south you will approach Captan Cook, Kealakekua Bay and eventually South Point, the southernmost point in the United States. The scenery is breathtaking with jagged cliffs and endless seas. Further on, you will encounter Green Sand Beach. It is made up of olivene, a semi-precious stone that gives the beach its incredible olive green color. There is a very rough trail that will take you to the top of the beach. It is unlink anything else in the world, but be prepared for a very long trek in. Once you reach the top of the beach trail, you must travel down another trail to get to the water. This is pretty remote and there are no facilities there, and no signs once on the trail. Whittington beach State Park and Black Sands Beach are also popular beaches in this area, and both have facilities. Turtles are often seen at Black Sands.

As you round the corner of the bottom of the island and return northwards on the windward side of the ocean, there are less beaches and beach parks. The water is rougher here, and there are multiple private beaches that are known only to locals who surf there. The sands here are mostly black, due to the volcano who has shaped this land, and many are not open to the public. Kalapana has a lave field park which ends at the sea. Although one cannot swim there, it is lovely to see where the lava ends and the sea begins. There is a small altar built on the lava by local Hawaiians. They are heads which represent the deities and ancestors, and is considered a holy place.

Volcanically heated tide pools, or thermal pools, provide good snorkeling and are a very popular spot to visit. Kapoho tide pools are a unique place to visit, swim, or snorkel. Another heated warm pond is at Ahalanui Park, also known as Pualla County Park. This looks like a large swimming pool, made of concrete with steps going down in to it, right next to the ocean. It is usually warm, but sometimes at high tide it can be a bit brisk as the ocean crashes over the barrier and mixes the cool and warm waters. Facilities are port-a-potties and an outdoor shower. At

Isaac Hale Park, off Pohoiki, near dead trees, is a hidden warm pool called 'Pele's Pond.' It is a rocky basin surrounded by trees with warm water. Small, but deep enough to swim around in, it is a natural jacuzzi next to a rough beach where surfing is popular. The contrast between the tranquility of the pool and the frenzy of the crashing waves make for an interesting contrast of senses..

Isaac Hale also has camping available and is a popular place to surf. Boats often launch from here, including those of the lava tours, which take people to the place where the lava meets the sea. It can be a rough place at times though, and theft is common, so please be mindful of your belongings while there.

Carlsmith Beach Park is lovely little beach park on the east side approaching HIlo. Tidal pools, lava rocks and scenic little inlets make this park one for both picnics as well as some swimming. Sandy, with some springs, there are sometimes cooler areas within the waters. Lovely place.

In Hilo Itself, there are many small parks. One is across from the Queen Lili'uokalani Park, which is a Japanese style park across from the Bay. There is an island park there, called Coconut Island, which is accessible via a bridge. Full facilities are there and people swim, and some snorkel. It is not unusual to see turtles there. Protected from the open ocean by the protected bay, this lovely place is used not only to swim, but for many cultural and community events. Sometimes you will find people working out in the evening as a group. Other times, it is used for Hawaiian cultural days where Hula and chanting are popular. It is a popular spot for many events, and festivals, including the fourth of July fireworks.

Also in HIlo you will find Wailoa State Park, with watery inlets, picnic pavilions, arched bridges and lots of open grassy spaces. Ducks are often seen at this fresh water park and the little lake empties in to the Wailoa River which passes the the King Kamehameha statue a few blocks away in an adjoining park. This small river is downside from where the government buildings are in Hilo. Across the street from that large, open park, is a beach front park that is not frequented. The waters are murky and people do not swim there. Closer to town is the bus stop, which is at the end of the park, and there is a pavilion there where musicians sometimes play.

Further up to the Hamakua coast there are many beautiful parks, but few that are safe for swimming. Some are very popular for surfing, such as Honoli'i Beach Park. This park has riptides and is not suitable for swimming, but to surfers the constant waves make it ideal. The inland portion of the park contains a stream which goes out to the ocean, and there is even a small water fall here. It is a nice place to picnic and for the scenery even if you do not surf.

Further up the Hamakua coast, you will find Onomea Bay. Onomea Bay is a stunning area with a botanical garden, waterfalls, and lovely scenery. Off of the Hawaii Belt Road, also known as Malama Highway, you will see a sign for the 'scenic drive' of four miles. Take it and you will encounter this lovely place, as well as other lovely sights. The botanical gardens boast an array of tropical flowers that will also leave your nose in paradise.

Further yet up the Hamakua coast you will encounter Laupahoehoe Point. This dynamic point is full of huge waves, lava rocks, cliffs and dramatic coastlines. There is a memorial here to a school house full of children who perished in a tsunami decades ago before warning systems were put in place. There are full facilities here and camping is allowed. The dramatic crashing waves make this no place to swim. There is a small boating ramp on the right side of the park, which some people do swim in, but the currents and the waves are high and dangerous here as well. Due your own due diligence and use your own discretion before entering these hazardous waters. It is a fierce and lovely place and is one of my favorite spots on the Hamakua coast.

Waipio Valley is between Hamakua and Kohala. Past Honokaa about nine miles, you will come to the Waipio Valley overlook. It is dramatic and stunning scenery, where whales play and kings once lived. This valley is considered sacred and to go down to the beach area requires a four wheel drive. Once one is down at the beach, please observe the sacredness of this land. The black sand beach is about a mile long, and is traversed through the middle by a river that is fed by the multiple waterfalls that drain into the valley, giving it its' unique lushness and vegetation. It is a watery world down there (and in fact the end of the movie 'Waterworld' was filmed here). The beach itself is a bit rough, but surfers surf here and people play. The river one must cross to get to the other side is only accessible by foot, no vehicles are allowed. It is all beautiful but once the river is crossed, it takes on an ethereal, primitive, vibe. Spirit is easily accessible here. The part of the river before you cross has plenty of parking, and port-a-potties for facilities, which are not always well kept. The valley north of Waimea are not accessible expect via boat or hiking in. The Kohala coast is on the other side of these valleys. We will resume our journey of selected beaches from the Kohala side, just south of where we began.

On the Kohala coast, there are multiple places to swim, but not all have facilities. Near the harbor, just past the Pu'ukohola heaiu,and Spencer Beach Park (where we began our description of selected beaches throughout the island) there are places to go and swim. You must check in at the security guard, in the road to the big harbor (you will see a huge port and many Matson shipping containers surrounded by fencing) and proceed in. Many families go there on holiday and barbeque, There is a concrete pad for boat access and ramps here. There are also structures in the water to climb on and jump off. On the left side, there is a pretty little secluded beach. There is a walkway that will take you up to the (Pu'ukohola) heaiu. Further down the coast is Kawaihae Harbor, a major industrial harbor followed by a normal sized one, which is a place where people swim, and also canoes are raced. They also hold church services on the beach at 5pm on the weekends there. Dive shops and whale watching cruises are also available here.

Further down the Kohala coast are multiple places where the ocean meets land, but few are amenable to swimming, due to rocks and high surf. They are great places to watch whales in the winter though, and many people frequent that side to have a picnic and to watch the whales. Often Maui is visible from that side as well. If you continue down to the 'end' of the road, you get the treat of a view of Honoka'a over the sacred Waipio and Waumano valleys from the 'opposite' side from which they are typically accessed. It is a truly beautiful place to see. Take the time to go to the overlook of the valleys and see the small islands that jut out to the sea in a fabulous display of nature's majesty. It is breathtaking.

This is but a small selection of various beaches throughout the island. After you are here a while you find which type of beach matches your style. Ask the locals which places they prefer for the activity your are thinking about. They may know of one of those hidden treasures which does not make it onto a map. Enjoy discovering your new home!

Chapter 10
Now that I Live Here -Now what?

Now That I Live Here - Now What?

You finally made it to your dream destination. Your pets and furniture are here and you've secured a job. No what? How do I connect with like minded people and projects that are dear to my heart? The answer depends on how you choose to create your life.

Churches and other Religious Organizations

Hawaii has multiple houses of worship. Catholic, Buddhist, Baptists, Latter Day Saints, Seventh Day Adventists, and Jehovah's Witness all have churches here. There are services on the beach at some places, and one place in Waimea is called Church Row due to the several churches of different denomination which occupy the same area. Churches support the feeling of community, and especially if you do not have children they will provide an anchor to your new neighbors. Try out a few if you do not currently belong to a particular organization and see what fits for you. You can keep on trying if nothing feels right. Eventually you will discover what works for you.

Schools

If you have children, you will automatically be plugged in to the community. Hawaii typically revolves around the keiki, the children, with entire communities coming out for sporting events and community events sponsored by the schools. There are also community colleges and The University of Hawaii. Take a class that interests you and you will find others who share your interests. Many communities offer adult learning to learn a new skill such as cooking, gardening, farming, handicrafts, or dancing. For both men and women, there is a large percentage of artistic people who enjoy sharing their talents. Life long learning is one key to a healthy life. By being open to new experiences your neural networks of your brain stimulate your body to stay sharper longer.

Sporting Events

Iron Man is a popular event held in Kona yearly. There are try outs and work outs for those interested in the intensity of that extreme sport. For those wo wish to stay is shape without the becoming a Iron Man or Woman, there are multiple local gyms, yoga and pilates centers and dance classes. In Hilo people sometimes gather on Coconut Island on some evenings when it is cooler to work out in groups. There are multiple trails to hike, and every community has high school sports. Even if you have no children in the school, you will get to know your neighbors by becoming part of the community that way. Community is important here.

Farmers Markets

Most communities also have local farmers markets run by local people. By frequenting these markets, not only will you get the best produce and products, but you will begin to know the local people who frequent the markets and man the stands. Many have music and dancing at these events. By being visible and friendly people will begin to recognize you.

Festivals

The festivals are places to come together and celebrate. Parades are community events, and even island events, binding the island community together. Many of the same vendors who frequent the farmers markets also participate at the festivals. Music is also part of most of these festivals, and no one care how you dance - just that you do and that you have fun! Go and enjoy.

Fraternal Organizations

If you are already a member of the Lion's Club, JayCees, or VFW, you will find a home immediately. If not, you are welcome to join a local organization that fits your interest. Many of these organizations participate in the parades and other fundraising events and are a big part of the community as well.

Country Clubs

If you are an avid golfer, consider becoming a member at the local country club or golf club. There are a wide variety of fees, but once you find one that fits your budget, you can make friends there. The 19th hole will also be a place one can find people of like mindedness.

Spiritual Events

There are many places of healing in Hawaii. Retreat centers abound and spas and classes for all sorts of practices can be found here. Reiki classes, crystal skulls, lomi-lomi massage, tarot, and meditation classes are available. Find one locally via Facebook or through the internet, or if you are intuitive, perhaps just wander into the place that calls you the most and have a fun experience!

Cultural Events

Hawaii still maintains an independence through their oral traditions, language, crafts, foods and traditions. Sometimes these events are open to non-Hawaiians. One can learn a lot about the history of the island this way, and also begin to build relationships with the other people who have found fascination with the Hawaiian culture. Many times the same people will frequent these events, and after a while become a social event for those who attend as well.

Science Projects

There is a community that participates in star gazing and other astronomical events. Hawaii is one of the best places in the world to observe space and the stars. There are several telescope on Mauna Kea and there is an observatory/ranger station part way up the mountain. They can tell you what type of events are planned.

Those with an interest in marine biology or just love the sea may volunteer to count whales during seasons. Opportunities vary, but often the University of Hawaii's marine biology programs are a good place to start to find out what projects are in need of volunteers. Sometimes there are social sites that show opportunities. Clean up campaigns are also popular and can be found on social media.

Become a Voice for Those who cannot Speak

One way to be part of the community is to become politically active and standing up for what you believe in. Many here support a GMO free environment and actively participate to have policy reflect the natural ways of the lands. Being an island, what happens here affects everyone. Pollutants in one area affect the rest of the island. It is important to have your voice heard if you live here. This may be protesting more building of telescopes on holy Mana Kea or voicing displeasure of the army's bombing the sites on the mountain, polluting the land, and disturbing the peace of the local residents. Speaking up for those who have no political (or human) voice are also options if they speak to you. It is your new home, speak up and be counted and make your voice heard.

Chapter 11
Some Final Thoughts

As you settle in to your new home, there are bound to be some transitions to make. As peaceful as this island is, there is at times an undercurrent of racism here, especially if you are white. Haole is the term for white people, it means 'without breath' or 'foreigner.' While the majority of the population has no problem with people of any color, there are some individuals who are still upset over the illegal overthrow of the monarchy, and blame outsiders, namely whites, for these troubles. Queen Lili'uokalani was held prisoner in her own palace and forced to give her country up to spare her people. Some feel the islands should revert back to the previous way of the monarchy, and become the Country of Hawaii as it once was.

The native Hawaiian people have several rights over this land that others do not. Cultural practices such as fishing, hunting, and collecting are some rights they legally have. Access to some holy grounds are also part of the rights instilled. Crown lands are given to those who can prove a certain percentage of Hawaiian lineage. Some are homesteads (lots), others are for agricultural or ranching use, in quantities of five to 500 acres. These lands are leased for 99 years and are able to be passed on to family who also possess the required amount of Hawaiian blood (currently at least 50% is required). There is a branch of government called OHA, the

Office of Hawaiian Affairs to oversee the management of these rights. This is analogous to the Office of Indian Affairs in the mainland. Hawaiian children now have Hawaiian schools and learn the language and culture of their ancestors. There is a cultural movement to reclaim Hawaii, and that is where as a newcomer, one must be sensitive. There has been great loss in the past, and it is embedded in the culture.

Being in a very strategic area of the Pacific, the military also has a presence here. Their presence is respected, but also incenses those who live near the land they bomb and have to deal with the aftermath of what seems to be a policy of the land being a disposable resource. It is also very noisy and disturbs the local wildlife, including the fish in the sea. This is mostly seen as arrogance as well as ignorance of the sacredness of the land.

This land is multi-cultural and is truly is a model of how to live together in peace. All different colors, races, lesbian, gay, transgender, straight, rich and poor all live together in peace, love, and tolerance. If you are understanding and sensitive, you will find great love and support here. Arrogance has no place here. If you are arrogant and insensitive, you will have a problem with the local people. The 'coconut wireless' will let people know about you long before you know about them. You may never know what is told about you. People generally do not talk to you directly about any indiscretions you may have unknowingly done. By being open and approachable, people will begin to tell you if you are not doing something 'the right way.' This all comes in time. By being yourself and doing what you love, you will fit in.

Hawaii is a land of 'your okay, I'm okay.' Just don't step on others toes while you do it.

Live in the spirit of aloha, and all will be well. People are truly friendly and full of love. Even those who pine for the old ways know it is nothing personal against you. Where there are drugs or alcohol involve sometimes mistakes in judgements can occur. Hawaii has the same drug problems as everywhere else, but the tolerance here of people's past allows new beginnings to happen. Even the prison system here is kind. It is re-enacting an ancient practice of sanctuary for those incarcerated on the mainland. It's aim is to bring them home and immerse them in their culture, including the Kahuna's presence and spiritual guidance. The thought is forgiveness, then reunion with the community will lead to skills to make a viable member of society.

Growing spiritually is something that happens here whether you plan on it or not. This mighty place supports the growth one needs to happen. May you grow in your spirit the love that conquers any past troubles and leads you to peace. Enjoy your new home in the land of aloha. Welcome home!

Epilogue

Now that you are settled in your new home, I hope you will take the time to let your voice be heard. Appreciate the land you now live on, and treat it with care. Living on an island it becomes very apparent that we are all interdependent upon each other and how we live affects all.

What ever part of the island you settle upon, you will notice that solar and wind power are present to help alleviate the dependence on outside fuels. Plastic bags are banned here to help with the toxicity caused by such materials, which also poison sea animals when carelessly tossed out to sea.

Being in such close proximity, it is easier to see how the actions of one can affect all. This is one reason why people on this island voice their opinions on subjects such as GMO foods, and the building of structures on sacred land.

As a resident who loves this land, you will most likely find an issue you are passionate about. Be it the health of the sea and the coral reefs, the endangerment of whales with explosions from undersea detonations, or mono cultured GMO crops which can threaten the flora here, if you see something that is not pono, not in right relationship, it is your kuleana, responsibility, to do something about it. Go to the meetings in Hilo or at the satellite offices of your local officials. They want to know what you think. If you disagree, state that as well. That is how policy is shaped. Being an island changes are seen quicker than on the mainland, so being vigilant is especially important.

We all depend on one another. As you shop at your local farmers market, not only do you get fresh local produce, you help the economy by keeping the money local. This helps all of us here to be more independent and self sustaining. As an island, the more that we can do ourselves, the better. This is one reason why solar and wind power, as well as charging stations for electric cars are common here. Freedom is clean and helps the environment. The less toxicity we can contribute to the nature, the better our lives will also be. The land can always restore herself, but we humans may not be around to see it if we keep up our toxic ways.

Buckminster Fuller called our living planet "Spaceship Earth." By this, he meant it is important to utilize our finite resources responsibly and for the good of all. There is abundant air, water, and life if we treat it right. Chances are you moved to Hawaii to be a part of this beautiful place, so it is imperative that you, as a resident, do what you can to keep it this way. As you love your new island home, and come to appreciate the distinct beauty and intricacy of this land, may your heart be opened as much as can be to let the light that shines within you out to bless all that it touches, this land, air and sea included.

Thank you for your willingness to be a part of this great community. You are welcomed in the spirit of aloha. Welcome home.

About the Author:

Dr Hostalek was born and raised near Chicago, but was open to exotic travel and mystical experiences from a young age. Mostly self-taught from a young age, her love of art and spirituality co-mingles in her art, books, and healing work. Most of her painting are made with holy water and contain the a vibrational essence of healing within them. She is a trained cranial osteopath and holistic physician, as well as a master ceremonialist, trained in the Andes and jungles of Peru, Equator, Mexico and England, by some of the best healers in this world. She has taught shamanic apprenticeships and continues to find joy in traveling, painting, and in helping others achieve their healing. She now makes her home on the Big Island of Hawaii, where she spends in days in spiritual communication with nature as she writes and paints, and does her healing work. For more information, to see her gallery of art, or to purchase her work please go to:

www.holisticwellnesshawaii.vpweb.com
or

www.starkeepersllc.com

Thank you!

Made in the USA
San Bernardino, CA
14 January 2014